Organise

Your Family

D1637593

Organise Your Family

From Chaos to Harmony

NICOLE AVERY

Wrightbooks
A Wiley Brand

First published in 2013 by Wrightbooks
an imprint of John Wiley & Sons Australia, Ltd
42 McDougall St, Milton Qld 4064

Office also in Melbourne

Typeset in ITC Berkeley Oldstyle Std Book 11/13.5 pt

Organise Your Family © Nicole Avery 2013

Excerpts taken from *Planning with Kids*, first published in 2011 by
Wrightbooks, an imprint of John Wiley & Sons Australia, Ltd

The moral rights of the author have been asserted

National Library of Australia Cataloguing-in-Publication data:

Author:	Avery, Nicole.
Title:	Organise your family: from chaos to harmony / Nicole Avery.
ISBN:	9781118626528 (pbk.)
	9781118678541 (ebook)
Subjects:	Families.
	Households.
	Home economics.
	Family life education.
Dewey Number:	306.85

Cover design by Susan Olinsky

Cover image: © iStockphoto.com/milalala

Printed in Singapore by C.O.S. Printers Pte Ltd

10 9 8 7 6 5 4 3 2

Disclaimer

Contents

About the author

Nicole Avery is the master organiser behind the popular blog 'Planning with Kids', where she shares tips and tricks to organising the chaos of family life.

Nicole is also a sought-after speaker and coach on areas from blogging and social media to home organisation and planning. She is mum to five beautiful kids.

Introduction

As a parent, I use planning as a safety blanket. When the chaos of daily life engulfs me, it's the constant in my life that lets me weave my way through all the school runs, the after-school activities, the washing, the cooking and the cleaning required to keep family life ticking along.

When I explain to people that I wasn't always an organised person, they're often surprised. Believe it or not, I grew up as a dawdling, absentminded, tardy kid—a point often raised by my family and oldest of friends! It's also amusing that my eldest son is just like I was—forever forgetting school notes, easily straying from a task and oblivious to the exasperation he causes me. At least I know it's possible to grow out of disorganisation, because that's exactly what I did.

When I was pregnant with our first child, I made plans to return to work after three months. Within a week of having our baby, I knew I wouldn't want to go back to work that soon. Luckily for me, my boss understood and allowed me to change my plan and return to work when my baby was nine months old.

I did feel guilty going back to work, even though I knew it was the right thing to do for my family at the time. I worked for just over 18 months before I went on maternity leave again with our second child. At the end of my 12 months' maternity leave in 2002 I had to decide whether I wanted to return to work or remain at home.

For the last three months of my maternity leave I became obsessed with deciding what to do. I loved being home with the kids, but part of me was scared of letting go of my career. What would I tick in 'Occupation' boxes? And how would I tell people what I did?

In the end, I knew we wanted to have more children, and I wanted to be at home at this stage of their lives. I moved beyond issues of title, other people's opinions and, most importantly, my own fear.

Almost 10 years later I'm technically back in the workforce deriving an income from my blog www.planningwithkids.com and I can control the hours I work around my family. There are moments when I wish I had more freedom (for example, going to the toilet on my own)—where I imagine myself walking out the door in the morning, reading the paper on the train, having a lunch break and spending full days away from the kids—but I know it isn't as simple as that. With working away from home comes the hassle of finding good childcare, the drop-offs and pick-ups, sick days, competing interests and worry.

If you're returning to work as a new parent or just thinking about how this could be done successfully, the tips and routines throughout the book can help you organise your daily workload so that getting out the door for work will be more manageable. Streamlining your everyday household jobs and getting the kids involved in the chores will ease your workload and decrease the morning rush-hour stress.

What I have learned through the 'working versus staying at home' dilemma is that whatever choice you make, it's important that you take happiness and wellbeing into account—not only the kids' and your partner's, but yours too. To take the best care of your family, you have to make sure you take care of yourself and are happy in what you're doing.

In growing our family of five children, the adjustment from one to two children was the hardest. Learning to cope with a newborn while having a toddler around was quite challenging, especially as the baby wouldn't sleep for more than 45 minutes during the day.

Throughout the first year of my second child's life, I often felt out of control and disorganised. It wasn't until I'd resigned from my job that I realised that to regain some sense of order and organisation I needed to apply the skills I'd used daily in the office to my family life. I couldn't plan all the things a baby or toddler would do during the day, but there was so much around the home that I could plan and prepare for.

This was a big moment for me. Being home fulltime was my new 'job' and, just as I would have done in my old job, I needed to find ways of improving the organisation of daily tasks. I'd made a shift from considering myself as not having a job to making my role as a mother my job, using all the skills I had to make life easier and more enjoyable for my family and myself. My first project was to get the evening meals under control as 5 pm had become a time of day that I dreaded. An overtired baby, a toddler wanting attention and a meal waiting to be prepared was a stressful and regular scenario.

It started out pretty small: I created a spreadsheet with all the meals I liked to cook and which the kids would eat. It listed each recipe, ingredients and instructions, and I could quickly generate a weekly shopping list of all the ingredients I needed for the week. No last-minute trips to the shops with children in tow as I had a comprehensive shopping list to work from. This single change to my routine made a significant difference to how I coped throughout the day. Most importantly, it increased my confidence in my own ability to be able to do my 'new job'. I couldn't make the baby go to sleep exactly when I wanted to or make him stay asleep once he'd finally nodded off, but I could easily plan and prepare for the evening meals.

My second project was to ensure I didn't become one-dimensional. Before I had children, I always had a number of interests outside of my work. I wanted to make sure that as a mum I could fit in time to enjoy interests outside of the home, so I set about doing this.

With the continuing support of my husband and two successful home projects, I had enough confidence in myself to know I'd not only cope with having more children, but I'd love it. And have more children we did! We're blessed to have five beautiful, happy, healthy kids with whom we live in a state of organised chaos. There is roughly a two-and-a-half-year gap between each child and the next in our family.

With each child I've learned more about how to be a mother and more about myself. As our family has grown I've read books, attended parenting seminars, listened to other parents and listened to my kids to help me find the best ways of managing daily family life. I've also developed strategies and processes to help me cope more ably with the workload that comes with a young family.

What I share in this book is the by-product of trial and error over more than a decade. Don't think it all runs perfectly at our house, because that's certainly not the case. There are days when I can hardly wait for the kids' bedtime to come around so I can have five minutes of peace and quiet. There are tears and fights that could have been prevented if I'd responded to certain situations differently. And there are those days when it all seems to go horribly wrong. Two fantastic things about parenting are that children are very forgiving and there's always tomorrow. When I get it wrong, I apologise to the kids, and they move on pretty quickly. Sometimes I wish I could move on as quickly as they do.

As a parent I've found small changes to household practices can make a massive difference to the harmony and balance of life. I hope this book will help you discover new ideas to enhance your organisation and allow more time for parenting.

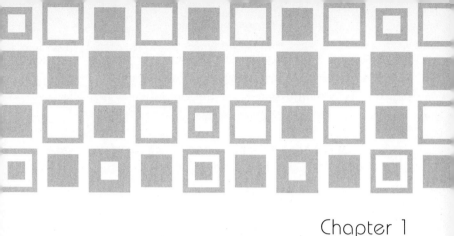

Chapter 1

Routines

Regular daily family life is full of repetitive and often boring chores. As our family has grown, I've learned a lot about being a parent and running a household. The most useful tip I've learned from my insight into parenthood has been to plan whatever you can so that when the unpredictable realities of family life arise they're much easier to cope with. This insight has been my main inspiration for creating simple routines and guidelines for managing our daily life. They've helped me to manage the high volume of repetitive household chores, and freed up time for more fun activities such as playing with the kids.

Establishing routines

Routines are like a comfort blanket for kids; they give them a sense of security. They let kids know what's coming up, what's expected of them and when it's expected, which helps to place boundaries around their big wide world.

Routines don't have to incorporate every waking minute of the day, but it's helpful if they cover the key activities that take place in daily life. For example, on school days there needs to be a more specific routine to ensure no-one is late, while on weekends and during school holidays routines can act more as a fluid framework around which to organise your day.

The best way to develop a routine for your family is to consider these key factors:

- your children's natural preferences
- regular family activities.

For example, in our house the kids are early risers, and this can often mean I start my day at 5 am! Instead of viewing this as a cross to bear, I use it to my advantage to kickstart our daily routine. In families with young children, giving yourself plenty of time to prepare the kids and everything else for school makes the mornings less stressful.

Our early morning routine also suits the children's natural preferences. Two of my school-aged children have a leisurely approach to getting ready. They like to have time to read or play and take things slowly in the morning so they get up early. If they got up half an hour before we leave the house, our mornings would soon become a battleground, with time and leisure competing fiercely. My other school-aged child is very different. His priority is to get himself ready and to be organised. He loves getting to school as early as possible so he has time to play before the bell rings, and he hates being late. This works beautifully in my favour as he's willing to help me and work cooperatively with the other children to ensure we leave the house on time.

Like most families with school-aged children, during the school term we have a number of after-school activities. There are activities such as dance classes, swimming lessons and footy training sessions to schedule in, and they help determine our weekly routine. As these activities can change each term, our routine needs to be modified regularly.

Unavoidable necessities have also helped shape our family routines. For example, over the past 11 years I've spent more time breastfeeding than not; therefore, this has been a big factor in determining our daily routine. As my husband has always worked reasonably long hours, I've had to juggle the bulk of the evening routine on my own. This is not something I've always found easy. There was often a tired toddler wanting attention or a grizzly baby in need of a calming feed competing for my time.

About six months into life with our second child, I decided I could better manage the baby's last feed of the day if I allowed our then 2 and a half year old to have his TV time while I breastfed. This system worked beautifully. The 30 minutes during which our toddler watched his pre-recorded show of *Playschool* allowed me to calmly give the baby his last feed of the day. I could then spend time with our toddler reading stories quietly while the baby was sound asleep.

Morning and evening routines are only two examples of routines you may have for your family. You may have a weekend routine where everyone sleeps in until after 7 am. (Well, to be honest, I added that one in as it sounds like heaven to me at the moment!) Or you may have a weekend routine where you go to the market to buy the fruit and vegetables for the week, or where you spend family time in the garden.

Whatever additional routines you have, make sure you have weekday morning and evening routines for the kids. It is at these busiest times of the day—the peak-hour periods of morning and evening—that you want your children to be able to operate with minimal direction and complete their chores as needed so they can move on to the next stage of their day or night. As with all aspects of parenting, though, common sense and flexibility are required when following routines. For example, if our preschooler has slept in after a late night, expecting him to complete all of his usual morning chores would be unreasonable. These instances, however, are the exception and not the rule, and routines can become a natural part of daily life for kids.

Morning routines

While getting organised and introducing routines may seem like a bit of work, the benefits of taking the time to do so are enormous as routines really do help manage the first rush hour of the day. A calm and happy start to the day is not only beneficial for the kids; it can set the tone for the adults' day too.

> Lay out your work clothes and child's clothes the night prior and pack a bag for childcare [to] leave at the door ready to go.
>
> **Kyrstie Barcak, mum of two**

Table 1.1 shows the morning routine my kinder and school-aged kids follow during the school term.

The younger children need a visual routine, which is a simple chart with pictures showing the order in which they should complete tasks when getting ready in the morning.

Table 1.1: school morning routine

Time	Task
6.00 am onwards	Breakfast
7.00 am	Breakfast table duties
7.30 am	Brush teeth; get dressed; apply sunscreen; tidy rooms
7.50 am	Pack bags
8.10 am	Leave house

Now, as fabulous as it would be if the kids looked at their routines and worked their way independently through them, this is not how it works in reality. However, with age they've become more practised at their routines and are able to complete tasks independently. There are still times when I need to provide guidance to ensure the kids get organised in the morning, but I'm not constantly having to nag at them as they know what they should be doing.

Getting kids organised in the morning

Preparing clothes

It's much less stressful to choose clothes for toddlers and preschoolers (in particular those who like to have a say in what they're wearing) the night before. My current preschooler has a couple of favourite T-shirts that are in constant rotation. Making sure they're available the night before, when there's no hurry to be out the door, makes choosing clothes much easier. Once the clothes have been selected they can be laid out and, if they're able, preschoolers can dress themselves in the morning just like their school-aged siblings.

I encourage the older children to be responsible for organising their own clothes. My husband and I

(continued)

Getting kids organised in the morning (cont'd)

currently do the laundry, but the older children put away their own clothes, so they should know exactly where they are (note the emphasis on should!). It still works best to have lower primary school children lay out their clothes the night before in readiness for the next day. Allowing upper primary school children to make their own choices about organising their clothes works well as it gives them a level of autonomy over their morning routines.

Key time markers

In the mornings we have key time markers. Time markers assist children in getting themselves ready and reduce the nagging that can take place at this time of the day. We have two key times on school mornings:

✓ 7.30 am: children have to have brushed their teeth and started getting dressed

✓ 8.00 am: we aim to leave the house at 8.10 am, so everyone should be almost ready.

School children, who can operate more independently, may just need a reminder about the time, but for the younger children a visual morning routine helps them work through the necessary steps.

School bags

Packing their own bags is an important task for building independence in preschool and school-aged children (and decreasing the workload of parents). Again, visual charts help to ensure that children have everything they need for their school day. For example, on days when they have library, they need to have their library bag and book; on sports days they need to take their runners to school.

Keep calm

This is probably the hardest one of these tips to consider some days! I find if I try to deal calmly with situations as they arise (rather than ranting and raving at the kids), there's much less chance of an issue escalating or snowballing into a larger tantrum or drama. From practical experience, I can highlight the benefits of staying calm. There will always be the occasional morning where the preschooler finds something else — such as playing with his toys — far more appealing than getting dressed. The way I approach this can determine how big the issue becomes. I can be:

✓ *frustrated*. I can tell him angrily to get ready, while moving the toys away from him. The preschooler then has a meltdown, and becomes even more uncooperative and unwilling to get himself dressed. This loud protest lasts for a considerable period of time, raising the stress levels of everyone in the house and putting pressure on us leaving the house on time.

✓ *calm*. This approach takes slightly longer, but it's worth the effort. I help the preschooler set aside what he's playing with, so he can come back to it later, and then help him get dressed. We may take turns at putting on his clothing: he does his underpants, I do his singlet, and so on. He may not be happy with having to stop playing, but we've avoided a complete tantrum.

Mornings can be a very busy time for families, and if parents have to direct all of their children's actions, this time of the day can quickly turn into a nagging session. By creating known and age-appropriate routines for the kids, you allow them to take on greater responsibility for getting themselves ready and, best of all, the parents don't have to nag so much.

Evening routines

When our eldest child was still a preschooler, we had the same evening routine every weekday as there weren't any after-school activities to worry about. How all that's changed now we have three children at school! Depending on your family's commitments, the second rush hour can begin as soon as the kids get home from school: homework to be completed, listening to reading, driving to and from after-school activities and trying to cook dinner while consoling an overtired toddler is a very common scenario at our house.

Our after-school routine varies greatly from one day to the next. However, one thing that doesn't change is having an early evening meal—dinner now just fits within a larger window than before we had kids at school.

Before children there are certain things you can't ever imagine yourself doing, and for me one of those was eating dinner at 5.30 pm. I had heard of people doing this and wholeheartedly scoffed at the idea. To me, 5.30 pm was still part of the day! Then, suddenly, I was home all day with two children, and on some days 5.30 pm seemed like midnight.

> When walking home from school in the afternoon I cut up beautiful apples for my children, which we eat as we walk. When we arrive home the children don't go to the pantry raiding the biscuits and bread as they are no longer starving and then they eat their dinner.

Georgina Rechner, mum of three

It didn't take me long to work out the reasons for and benefits of eating dinner at 5.30 pm with the kids.

- Kids are actually hungry at this time.

- Kids eat better when they're not overtired, and tiredness really starts to kick in for babies, toddlers and preschoolers after this time.

- With this tiredness comes a significant drop in kids' attention spans and their ability to sit still at the table, making mealtimes less enjoyable.

- Meals are a social time for kids too. Actually sitting down and eating a meal with them is a wonderful chance to connect and talk about their day.

Having an evening routine is also one of the best ways of getting children into bed at a reasonable time with a minimum of fuss, which increases family harmony: if kids sleep well, they're more likely to eat well; if kids are well rested and eat well, they're more likely to behave considerately and cooperatively.

> At bedtime, the routine is important (dinner, wash, bed, books). What time these happen and how long they take is less important. The concept of time, which is abstract, is not relevant to kids until they are 8+ but the sequence of events is learnt early.
>
> **Julie Holden, mum of two**

While our evening routine won't suit all families (because everyone has different after-school and work commitments), table 1.2 (overleaf) is included as an example of the way an evening routine can work. This was our routine when our youngest child was still a baby.

Table 1.2: evening routine

Time	Activity
5.30 pm	Dinner
6.00 pm	Bath and showers
6.20 pm	Put on pyjamas
	Take care of dirty washing; clean up bathroom; tidy up (general)
6.30 pm	Younger children (six and four years old): technology/TV time
	Older children (11 and nine years old): reading and homework
	Baby: breastfeeding (if nine year old has finished homework, then I read his story as I feed the baby)
7.00 pm	Baby goes to sleep
	Younger children: brush teeth, toilet, story and song
	Older children: technology time
7.30 pm	Younger children go to bed
	Older children: technology/TV time
8.00 pm	Nine year old: brush teeth, toilet, story, bed
	11 year old: additional technology time
8.30 pm	11 year old: brush teeth, toilet, bed

Working parents can record talking books or videos for children so they can still be part of the bedtime routine.

Julie Holden, mum of two

Getting kids into bed calmly

✓ *Aim for consistent times.* Starting the bedtime routine at a similar time each night means the kids get to know when they're expected to be in bed. This familiarity makes bedtime easier to manage as children don't have an expectation that they can stay up until they feel like going to bed.

✓ *Have winding-down signals.* The steps in a bedtime routine act as signals to the kids that it's time to slow down and prepare for going to bed. Repeating the same steps each night is important so the kids can tune in to the signals. It's difficult to get children to fall asleep instantly without any time to wind down and relax.

✓ *Read a story.* I've found this to be a very enjoyable part of the bedtime routine for our family. Days can be very busy and it's easy for them to pass by without making time to read a story. Having this as part of our bedtime routine ensures we do read a story together every day and gives the kids a chance to relax before going to sleep.

✓ *Create a calm atmosphere.* When the bedtime routine begins, it's a good idea to turn off distractions such as the TV, computers and loud music. This brings a level of quiet to the house, which is calming for young children.

✓ *Prepare the bedrooms.* Plan for bedrooms to be tidy before story time. This is not the time to start tidying bedrooms or making beds; this is the final wind-down stage of the day, so don't create a whirlwind of activity.

Slotting cleaning into your routine

I'll be completely honest and say that cleaning is my least favourite aspect of daily life. People often think that as I'm slightly planning obsessed I must have the 'perfect' house, but I'm always happy to dispel this myth! My house is generally well organised, but with five children it meets that 'perfect' status only on very rare occasions, and even then only after a tremendous amount of work.

Rather than aspire to perfection, therefore, I've instead found a base level of cleanliness and tidiness that I need to operate from. This was an important discovery for me, not just because it mattered to me what the house looked like, but also for controlling my stress levels! Over the years I've worked out that when the piles of papers start to build up, the toilets need cleaning (very regularly with lots of boys in the house) and the floors need a vacuum and mop, my underlying stress levels increase. From this elevated baseline of stress, I found my patience was shorter, I would find more faults in what my very patient husband was doing and all I could see was mess everywhere I looked.

> Every morsel that passes my children's lips MUST be consumed at the table. Otherwise I spend my day sweeping or cursing the amount of crumbs and food rubbish littered throughout the house. We always have a face washer sitting on the kitchen sink to wipe the children's hands and mouth.
>
> **Katie McIntosh, mum of eight**

This scenario would inevitably end with my having a massive rant about the filthiness of the house and how I was tired of cleaning all the time (and so on and so on—a scenario that's probably very familiar to most mothers. I realised there are key household chores that, when under control, I can turn a blind eye to (such as bookshelves that need dusting or a dirty oven).

A key task guide

One of my biggest discoveries as a stay-at-home mum was that not only do kids function better with routines, but so do parents. Daily life can be so busy it can be overwhelming at times. A common reaction to feeling overwhelmed is paralysis: doing nothing because you don't know where to start.

Whenever I was overwhelmed by the amount of cleaning needing to be done, it showed in a couple of very obvious ways. I would walk from room to room, picking up stuff here and there with no real purpose; or I would start a job only to be distracted midway by something as simple as the books on the bookshelf needing to be straightened. To remedy this situation I created a basic cleaning routine. The routine outlines the first tasks I should work on each morning after the school drop-off. Once I get going, I quickly find my rhythm and make my way through the house, but having a starter task has proved invaluable. Table 1.3 shows exactly what I mean.

Table 1.3: key task guide

Monday	Tuesday	Wednesday	Thursday	Friday
Cook evening meal	Toilets and basins	Cook evening meal	Laundry	Toilets and basins
Benches	Laundry	Vacuum	Benches	Vacuum
Vacuum				

This routine lets me switch to autopilot. I can come in from the school run each weekday morning and know which task to tackle straight away. For example, if we have swimming lessons after school on Mondays, I know my key task on Monday morning is to prepare the evening meal. Having it prepared early helps make the after-school rush much more manageable. If our preschooler and toddler are not able to amuse themselves and need my attention I put the other key tasks for the day on hold and play with the kids. I then try to find other blocks of time during the day to complete them. Just after lunch when the kids have been refuelled is often a good time for catching up on unfinished tasks.

The key tasks are my priority prompts—they keep me on track. However, they're not all of my day's tasks. There are days when I don't follow this routine at all as we may have appointments, play dates or other higher priority tasks. However, the guide is imprinted in my head and if there aren't any other commitments, I can move straight on to purposeful work without having to think about it.

The 15-minute block

Prior to having children, I used to love the feeling of sitting on the couch and looking around the house knowing that *everything* had just been cleaned. I still remember that lovely feeling, but after my second child was born I finally gave up the idea of trying to clean the entire house in one day. With feeding, playing and napping to juggle the cleaning around, it simply wasn't a realistic objective.

When I had only two children I worked on a system where I'd break down the house cleaning into rooms. I'd complete one room at a time and make my way through all of the rooms in the house over one week. Then along came baby number three, baby number four and baby number five! It was after our last child was born that I had another realisation—my objective of cleaning whole rooms at a time might work occasionally (depending on the sleeping pattern of the baby and the mood of the preschooler), but it wasn't a routine I could depend upon to successfully clean the house.

Thankfully, at this time I also came across the very practical concept of working in 15-minute blocks. It wouldn't be going too far to say that this revolutionised my approach to cleaning and, more importantly, gave me the feeling I was staying on top of things. I highlighted my key tasks in table 1.3 (see p. 13) and you can see that—with the exception of cooking the family meal—all of these tasks can be completed in 15-minute blocks. This works for the following reasons:

- The children can easily occupy themselves for this length of time.

- Starting a task you know you can complete without having to stop halfway through can give you a feeling of achievement even when you feel there's just too much to cope with.

- This amount of cleaning makes an instant difference to the tidiness and/or cleanliness of the house.

- If you don't love cleaning (and not many of us do), it's easier to stick to a single task knowing that it will only take 15 minutes.

Once I arrive home from the school drop-off, I start my first 15-minute block for the day (apart from the days when cooking is my first key task, in which case I begin with that even if it takes longer than 15 minutes). I set my toddler and preschooler up with an activity and then hop straight into it. If I've completed one 15-minute block and the children are still happily playing, I move swiftly on to another one.

Look at your daily routine and find places where you can slot in 15-minute cleaning blocks. The more house cleaning becomes part of your daily routine, the more likely you are to get it done. Fifteen-minute blocks work best when you can fit them around constant events in your day such as:

- before leaving to take the kids to school
- after school drop-off in the morning
- before putting your toddler to bed
- before school pick-up in the afternoon
- while the kids are having afternoon tea.

There are numerous cleaning activities that can be completed in 15 minutes. Here's a list to get you started:

- picking up and packing away anything that's not in its place
- cleaning toilets
- wiping bathroom benches, basins and mirrors
- wiping down kitchen cupboards
- dusting one room
- vacuuming the main living areas
- putting on, hanging out, folding a load of washing
- emptying and cleaning bins
- changing bed linen
- cleaning the windows in one room.

Involving the family

Although I'm the primary cleaner in our house, this doesn't mean I should be responsible for everything! As part of our family's weekly routines I've made sure there are plenty of opportunities for my kids and husband to contribute to the upkeep of our family home.

Getting the kids to help

It's important that children don't think a 'clean-up fairy' lives in their house. If you continually remove the rubbish from their bedrooms or take the dirty clothes to the laundry for them, kids won't learn how much work these jobs involve. By delegating some responsibility to each child, not only will you make them aware of the work involved in keeping the household running smoothly, but they will also learn valuable independence and life skills.

For me, this means that sometimes I have to live with some mess and untidiness until the kids get home from school and clean up after themselves. This can be hard to do when you have to walk past their bedrooms a number of times a day and see the mess scattered all over the floor, so now I close the doors until the kids are home.

Starting kids off early with age-appropriate jobs is the best way to get them involved with the cleaning and daily household chores. Table 1.4 shows an example of age-appropriate tasks. Note that it assumes an add-on approach where, for example, 11 year olds would be doing some of the tasks from each age group below them as well as the tasks appropriate for their age.

Table 1.4: children's age-appropriate tasks

Age	Tasks
2–3 year olds The aim is not for perfection, but for children to begin learning to do things for themselves and to contribute to the running of the family home. They will need assistance.	■ Take breakfast dishes away from table. ■ Make bed and tidy room. ■ Wipe and sweep up own messes throughout the day. ■ Pack away toys and generally tidy up. ■ Take condiments to table for evening meal. ■ Take own plate away from dinner table. ■ Place dirty clothes in laundry basket. ■ Return towel to bathroom.

(continued)

Table 1.4: children's age-appropriate tasks (*cont'd*)

Age	Tasks
4–5 year olds The aim is for children to know their own job routines and to carry them out without having to be reminded. They may still need some assistance.	■ Return cereal boxes to cupboard after breakfast. ■ Pack kinder bag or school bag. ■ Unpack kinder bag or school bag and hand over any notices. ■ Set place mats for dinner. ■ As required, help match up socks when laundry is being folded. ■ Assist in the garden with sweeping and raking.
6–7 year olds The aim is for children to now be completing their tasks independently.	■ Place milk and juice back in the fridge after breakfast. ■ Empty rubbish bins. ■ Set cutlery for dinner. ■ Put own laundered clothes away. ■ On weekends, help make morning and afternoon tea. ■ Cook treats such as scones and muffins. ■ Help sort laundry into colour groupings.
8–10 year olds The aim is for children to be taking on tasks that require more time, and to complete a household task rather than only a part of it.	■ Stack dishwasher. ■ Empty compost bin and clean container. ■ Make drinks for evening meal. ■ Vacuum own bedroom. ■ Help cook a family meal as required. ■ Assist with folding clean laundry. ■ Help with weeding the garden.
11–12 year olds The aim is to have a variety of indoor and outdoor jobs for children of this age.	■ Unstack dishwasher. ■ Vacuum whole house as required. ■ Regularly cook a family meal by themselves. ■ Mow lawn. ■ Hang out washing. ■ Put away groceries.

It's important that the job of cleaning the family home isn't left to any one individual. Take time to divide up the workload and include house cleaning as part of your family's daily routines. Giving every family member some responsibilities appropriate for their age will contribute towards keeping the house at a level of cleanliness and tidiness you can cope with.

Getting your partner to help

I'm fortunate to have a husband who helps keep the house clean and tidy. This, however, wasn't always the case, and it's been a transitional change. I found the way to reach an agreement with my husband where he would contribute more to the household upkeep was to do the following:

- Discuss my expectations and needs with him.

- Allocate him set tasks (anyone can work well with a routine!).

- Realise that he doesn't see what I see. So, if a job needs doing, I have to ask him to do it rather than martyr myself by doing it in a huff!

- Give him space to complete a task and accept that he may not do it the way I do (I still find this a bit hard, but I'm working on it!).

- Teach him about 15-minute blocks.

Taming the laundry beast

There's no bigger part of daily life for a growing family than doing the laundry. As you can probably imagine, with five children we generate a significant amount of washing. Naturally, this results in a large amount of folding and ironing, and I admit to not always having it under control. After a particularly busy week, you'll see a mountain of clean washing needing attention in our front room. I still manage to get the washing done (out of necessity), but if time is tight, the folding in particular tends to be neglected. The flow-on effect of not having the washing up to date is never very pretty — 'Mum, where are my footy shorts?'; 'Mum, where are my school socks?') — so the incentive to keep it in check is considerable.

> After number eight I gave up ironing. I have a fantastic washing machine and dryer. I now hang very little on the clothes line. I realise this is environmentally irresponsible but it's great for my sanity and the washing turnover.
>
> **Katie McIntosh, mum of eight**

In table 1.3 (see p. 13), you'll see I've included laundry on Tuesdays and Thursdays. Like most mums with a large family, I usually do the washing every day, but these are the two days when I *have to* make sure I do a load of washing. The school children have two sets of school uniforms and one sports uniform each. They all have sport on Thursdays, so from their school schedule I know that for them to have clean uniforms I must wash on Tuesdays and Thursdays. It's been helpful to note this, so when we have super busy days and are out and about a lot, I know on which days I need to do a load of washing.

I like to determine my minimum requirements so I can adequately plan my week to fit them in. This can be just a mental note allowing me to operate on autopilot. Being able to function on autopilot can be incredibly important when you have young children, particularly when you're sleep-deprived or coping with several sick kids. It means you can still meet your minimum requirements (in this case having clean clothes) to keep daily life humming along without having to spend time working out what it is you have to get done.

Keeping the laundry tasks under control

Here is a collection of my tips and also tips from other mothers who kindly shared them with me on my blog. Not all of them will suit your family, but there are fantastic strategies listed here that will allow you to tame the beast that is the family laundry pile.

✓ Avoid letting it build up. Aim for daily loads as it's always worse when you are knee-deep in dirty clothes.

✓ If you have a timer function on your washing machine, load the machine up the night before and set the timer so the washing is ready when you come home from the school run.

✓ Hang more delicate clothes such as business shirts on hangers and fold the rest of the clothes as neatly as possible in a basket to reduce the amount of ironing.

Deb Hodgkin, mum of two, www.science-at-home.org

✓ Aim to fold clothes that don't need ironing as soon as you take them off the clothes horse or clothes line rather than putting them back in a basket.

✓ Involve the kids and your partner in sharing the workload.

Holding family meetings

We've been using family meetings as a tool for managing and planning our life for more than eight years now. For our family, the aim of family meetings is to:

- provide an organised way of dealing with contentious issues
- create a forum where all voices are equal
- create a space where we can jointly plan fun activities and other parts of home life
- role model and offer opportunities for the kids to practise decision making, negotiation and problem-solving skills
- create a sense of ownership of family decisions.

During the meetings we try to encourage the kids to take part in solving problems and generating ideas. If a child has an issue they want raised at the family meeting, they have to bring along a solution and not just the problem.

We started having family meetings when our eldest child was four and our second child was two. When you only have children of this age at a family meeting, it can feel slightly strange! However, starting the meetings with kids at this age means they'll grow up accepting them as part of their life: they'll expect to have meetings regularly, and will be prepared to contribute their thoughts and opinions.

Guidelines for family meetings

We developed guidelines so everyone would understand how family meetings were to be run. Depending on the age of your kids and your family dynamics, our guidelines may not necessarily be a perfect match, but you can use the key headings that follow to develop your own guidelines for providing a strong framework for your family meetings.

Set a time and frequency

Set a regular time and day when everyone is most likely to be at home. Decide how often you want to meet. (We currently meet fortnightly.)

Choose a suitable place

The meetings need to be held in a place that's free from distractions. (We use the dinner table.)

Decide who should attend

All family members over the age of two are expected to attend our meetings.

Rotate the convenor or chair

At our place we take it in turns to convene meetings so that everyone has a go. Mum or Dad assists the toddler and preschooler until they get the hang of things.

Take minutes

We take minutes at each meeting and these are always reviewed as the first agenda item at the next family meeting. The children who can write also have a turn at taking the minutes.

Choose a time frame

Due to the age of the children attending, we aim to make our meetings last no longer than 20 minutes.

Raise hands

Everyone must raise their hand and be acknowledged by the convenor before they may speak. This practice teaches children that in meetings not only do you have an opportunity to talk, but you also need to listen to others.

Follow agenda items

Although we use a formal structure for our family meetings, they're generally lighthearted and fun. Quite often the meeting is more of a sharing time, where kids or adults provide updates to the family on areas of their life or items of interest.

Ensure agreement

We keep working on a resolution for each matter raised until we have one that all family members can agree on. This is critical to the success of our family meetings. No-one should leave the family meeting feeling they haven't been listened to or their needs haven't been taken into consideration.

The benefits of family meetings

Our regular family meetings have allowed us to establish a forum for resolving problems and sharing ideas. When an issue arises in the middle of a busy day it can be very helpful if I can assure everyone I'm putting the matter on the agenda for the next meeting. It instantly takes the heat out of the situation and makes the kids start thinking about solutions.

Family meetings allow for all family members to feel their contribution has been taken into account, regardless of their age. This doesn't mean the kids get exactly what they want, but it teaches them about compromise and that sometimes getting agreement means making concessions. It also teaches the older children to work out what are the 'must-haves' in relation to their issues, and makes them practise using persuasive arguments to attain what they want. Most importantly, as the kids have had an input regarding the decisions being made at family meetings, there's a much better chance they'll stick to those decisions in the future.

Taking action

- Establish morning and evening routines for your children.

- Determine your base operating level of cleanliness and tidiness for the family home.

- Create a key task guide that will help you maintain this base level.

- Complete your key tasks using 15-minute blocks of activity.

- Allocate household chores to every member of the family as part of their daily routines.

- Determine your minimum requirements for laundry across the week and incorporate them into your key task guide.

- Use family meetings as a tool for managing and planning daily family life.

Chapter 2

Meals

Meals play a large part in family life. As parents, we have to think about what to feed the kids and when; we have to buy and prepare the food; and then we have to try to get the kids to eat what we've cooked! This aspect of daily life can take up significant amounts of time and can also cause considerable stress. But it doesn't necessarily have to be that way. One of my biggest realisations as a parent has been that it's worth the effort of taking time to plan meals. It has reduced the amount of time I spend on meals and has helped make mealtimes a more enjoyable part of the day.

Menu planning

Menu planning helps solve the dreaded question that arises at about 4 or 5 pm every day: 'What's for dinner?' Before having kids, I would rarely give a thought to dinner until I arrived home from work. I would even make a quick trip to the supermarket to buy additional ingredients if I felt like having something special.

With several children, there's no such thing as a quick trip to the supermarket. Nor is it always an easy job to cook with small children hanging off your hips and legs. As I mentioned at the start of the book, menu planning was one of the first projects I set myself when I decided to take a more prepared approach to organisation at home. It's the best way to streamline a very repetitive task and create order during a busy part of the day.

Family menu plans can be as brief or as detailed as you like. A menu plan covers every day of the week and all the meals you intend to cook for the family. If you're very eager, you can plan breakfast, lunch, dinner and snacks for the whole day. I've never found the need to go this far, so I just document what our evening meals will be each day of the week. Once I've chosen our meals I can easily prepare a shopping list to make sure I'll have all the required ingredients on hand.

I plan the meals at the start of the week on the whiteboard on the fridge so what I want is defrosted by the time I get home from work. I cook a double lot of things like a casserole or spaghetti sauce using the slow cooker, then freeze half in small portions (quicker to defrost or just defrost as much as you need and fit[s] in the freezer better).

Marita Shepherd, mum of two

Why menu planning works

In essence, menu planning works because it saves you time. As with a lot of other tasks, the thought of sitting down and planning is actually worse than the deed itself. Once you get going you can quickly choose meals for your family. It actually takes a lot less time than if I were to consider the question, 'What will we have for dinner?' every single day.

Menu planning is another system that allows you to run on autopilot in the middle of busy days with the kids or at work. The hard work of thinking about what to cook has been done, so in the lead-up to mealtime it's just a matter of referring to the meal plan and then cooking. The additional bonus of menu planning is it also helps with other areas of daily life.

- *It saves money.* By planning the meals for the week you can purchase all the ingredients you need at one time. No more rushed trips, where you end up buying much more than intended. Planning allows you to take advantage of supermarket specials by selecting meals that use ingredients which are on sale.

- *It supports healthy eating.* As you have the ingredients on hand and have already thought about what to cook, you're much less likely to substitute your planned meal for takeaway or a less healthy home-cooked option (like toast!).

- *It decreases stress levels.* The late afternoon and early evening time with small children can be fraught with overtiredness, tears and whining. To then have to think of what to cook and perhaps even have to leave the house to purchase ingredients can really increase stress levels. Menu planning eliminates this source of stress from the equation.

- *It supports regular eating as a family.* If meal planning is left to the last minute, it can be very tempting to whip something up quickly for the kids and then have to organise a separate meal later for the adults. By having planned what to cook, you're much more likely to sit and eat with the kids.

■ *It offers variety.* Planning your family's weekly meals means you can ensure efficient use of food yet still keep variety by using the same ingredients in different combinations.

An instant guide to menu planning

I've been menu planning regularly for about eight years and I've finetuned the process I use. I now menu plan on a monthly basis, but the process can be applied to any time frame. These are the steps I follow.

Step 1: decide on a daily theme

Choose a style or category of meal for each day of the week. This makes planning for periods longer than a week much easier and quicker. My standard categories are:

■ pasta-based dishes

■ meals with rice

■ slow-cooker meals

■ bulk meals (I use the leftovers from these for other meals)

■ quick meals (up to 15 minutes of preparation)

■ meals that my husband and the kids can cook

■ meat and vegetables

■ soups

■ vegetarian.

> We have a number of easy and quick meals that we do on the nights that I have been working, such as tacos or tuna mornay, so that the kids don't have too long to wait between getting home and eating. I decide what meal we will be having the night before so that I can make sure I defrost the meat or buy any ingredients that we may need.

Leona Campitelli, mum of three

Once I've taken into account after-school activities, weather and weekend commitments, I allocate each of the categories to a day of the week.

- *Monday:* pasta-based dish (gymnastics from 4 pm to 5 pm)
- *Tuesday:* slow-cooker meal—cooking can be done earlier in the day (swimming from 5.30 pm to 6.00 pm)
- *Wednesday:* meal with rice (football training from 5.30 pm to 6.45 pm)
- *Thursday:* bulk meal (often by Friday I really don't feel like cooking so a bulk meal on Thursday is good preparation)
- *Friday:* leftovers (football training from 4.30 pm to 5.30 pm)
- *Saturday:* meals that my husband or the kids can cook
- *Sunday:* meat and vegetables (football at 8.45 am and 11.00 am).

Step 2: consider seasons and specials

Fresh fruit and vegetables are always much tastier and cheaper when they're in season. I find out which fruits and vegetables are in season and take this into consideration when selecting meals. I also use the supermarket catalogues for inspiration, checking out which key ingredients are on special and selecting meals that use them for our menu plan. I note these down to start the list of meals that I'll choose from.

Step 3: get input from the family

My kids are quite used to my menu planning. When I have a monthly menu-planning session, I ask them to suggest up to four meals they'd like included.

There are three key benefits to involving the kids.

- They're happier to eat the meals as they know their favourite meal is coming up too.

- It provides opportunities to talk about seasonal food; for example, why we don't often eat casseroles in summer and which vegetables are in season.

- It means I have to choose fewer meals myself!

I also hunt down my husband to see whether he has any requests for our evening meals. I write everyone's suggestions on my growing meal list.

Step 4: allocate the meals

Now I have a comprehensive list of meals to choose from. I use a monthly template to slot meals against the relevant days so they fit into the daily categories I've selected. As mentioned earlier, you can plan for any time frame; however, I've found monthly to be the optimal period for our family. Having done this so many times now, I can plan our meals for the month in 35 minutes. The end result can be seen in table 2.1. You can download a monthly menu planning template at www. planningwithkids.com/resources.

Table 2.1: monthly menu planner

Week beginning	Monday: Pasta	Tuesday: Slow cooker	Wednesday: Meal with rice	Thursday: Bulk meal	Friday: Leftovers	Saturday: Kids or Dad	Sunday: Meat and veggies
2 August	Penne bake	Chicken noodle soup	Beef stir fry	Mexibake	Leftovers	Chicken wings and baked potatoes	Roast lamb and veggies
9 August	Pasta with chicken and spinach	Beef stroganoff	Tuna rice	Chicken schnitzel and steamed veggies	Leftovers	Souvlaki	Chicken schnitzel and steamed veggies
16 August	Spaghetti bolognaise	Pumpkin soup	Moroccan minted beef	Shepherd's pie	Leftovers	Tacos	Roast beef and veggies
23 August	Pasta carbonara	Beef curry	Spicy chutney chicken	Pasties	Leftovers	Fried rice	Sausage and veggies

Shopping for growing families

Once I've created a menu plan, not only has this made mealtime easier, but the task of shopping for groceries has now been simplified too. The menu plan allows me to easily collate a shopping list to take to the supermarket.

Shopping lists

Shopping lists are the key to efficient shopping for our family. I have two options for creating a shopping list: I can manually scan the meals I've chosen into the menu plan and write up a list; or, I can use a free menu planner tool such as the one provided on the blog. Go to www.planningwithkids.com/menuplanner/index.php. This menu planner has a simple, five-step procedure:

1   Select the date for the beginning of the week.

2   Choose your meals.

3   Choose the number of serves required for each meal.

4   Tick the boxes of the recipes you wish to print out.

5   Print out the menu plan, recipes and shopping list.

The shopping list is arranged by food type, making the task of finding the items you need when you're at the supermarket quicker and easier. As the menu planner only looks at the evening meals, our shopping list is still a work in progress and needs to have other groceries and household items added to it. To help build a comprehensive shopping list that ensures no last-minute rushed trips to the supermarket, there are a couple of other lists I refer to:

■   *Pantry checklists.* I have checklists stuck to the inside of the pantry cupboards. As I run out of items or items are close to running out, I place a tick next to them on the checklists. When it comes time to write my shopping list, I simply add the ticked items to it.

- *Lunchbox items.* Fresh fruit and vegetables are the easiest way to fill the kids' lunchboxes. To retain some variety, I refer to lists of seasonal fruit and vegetables that I know the kids will eat.

Where to shop

Living in a capital city, I'm lucky to have several options when it comes to shopping for our family groceries. My shopping routine over the past few years has consisted of a monthly online grocery shop, a monthly visit to the butcher and a weekly trip to a fresh fruit and vegetable market. Not all of these may be available where you live, but it's worth considering them if they are.

Online shopping

The first time I shopped online it took me ages, and I thought it was a very time-consuming process. However, it's really only slow the first couple of times you do it—after that it's a super-efficient way to shop because of the following reasons:

- All your previous orders are listed and you can quickly tick the items you wish to add to your trolley the next time you shop.

- You can buy in bulk because the goods are delivered to your door.

- You can see exactly how much you're spending and either remove or add discretionary items so you stay within your budget.

- You can easily compare prices as products can be listed by unit price.

- You can do it on your own!

Markets

We shop weekly at a nearby market, and have found that buying fruit and vegetables at markets is significantly cheaper than purchasing them from the supermarket. In addition, the quality is far superior. If you haven't tried a market, consider these tips for your first visit.

- Take with you a list of prices for the items you buy regularly from the supermarket so you can compare.

- Allow yourself plenty of time to walk around the market first to note the varying prices and quality of the produce. Even at markets you'll find stallholders who don't offer value for money.

- Go back and make your purchases, noting how much you pay and the location of the stall that you bought them from. If you know the location of the stalls you like, this will make the process quicker next time.

- When you get home, do some quick calculations to see how much you saved. It can be more of an effort to go to a market than to the local shops, so having a concrete dollar amount can be a great incentive to keep up the habit. Table 2.2 illustrates how much you could save on your grocery bill by going to the market.

Butcher

For a number of years I worked on the false assumption that because supermarkets have chains they should be able to deliver cheaper prices on meat. I was very much mistaken. Meat is often very expensive at the main supermarkets in Australia. From my experience, I've also found the quality of meat superior at a local butcher shop. Not all butchers are cheap, so I spent some time comparing prices and quality and have found a local butcher shop that provides great meat at a great price. When looking for a local butcher, consider the following points:

- Do they offer discounts for bulk purchases? For example, chicken breasts are $3.00 per kilogram cheaper if I buy more than two kilograms at a time.

- Can you can ring in your order and pick it up later? This is a great convenience when you're shopping with little ones.

- Do they have regular specials you can take advantage of (not all of them do)?

- Is there a market near you that sells meat? Big markets such as the Queen Victoria Market in Melbourne — and (increasingly) farmers markets throughout the country — are selling local meat at great prices.

Table 2.2: market savings

Item	Supermarket	Market	Quantity	Saving
Red capsicums (kg)	$6.99	$3.99	1.5	$4.50
Apples (kg)	$4.98	$2.50	5	$12.40
Carrots (kg)	$2.29	$1.49	2.5	$2.00
Pumpkin (whole)	$2.99	$2.00	2	$1.98
Lettuce (iceberg)	$2.99	$1.99	1	$1.00
Total				**$21.88**

Discount retailers and warehouse clubs

In recent years, Australia has seen the introduction of a number of international stores such as Aldi and Costco. They can help you save significant amounts of money, but you should keep the following in mind:

■ *Buy only what you need.* Cheap is tempting, but remember to stick to your list.

■ *Buy in bulk.* I love buying items in bulk as this offers great value (when I know we'll use everything). To make the most of bulk buying, consider teaming up with a friend and sharing the goods if the discounts only apply for large volumes.

■ *Be prepared to try new brands.* Don't expect to see all your familiar brands at these stores. I've tried different brands for products such as tomato paste, pasta sauces, plastic wrap, chocolate and nappies and have found the quality comparable.

■ *Factor in the extra fees.* Some of these stores have surcharges for credit cards. There can also be costs for purchasing bags, as well as membership and parking fees that you might have avoided elsewhere.

■ *Add up the transport costs.* Did you have to pay tolls to get there, and how much petrol did it cost?

Enjoying your mealtimes

With our meals selected and ingredients bought, we're halfway towards enjoying a family meal. Most evenings (life is never perfect!) we sit down together to eat our dinner and enjoy each other's company. As we eat early in the evening from Monday to Friday, only I eat with the kids. Then, on the weekends, my husband is around to eat with us.

Here are some tips on how to make mealtimes more enjoyable for everyone, based on my past experience.

Involve the kids in menu planning

Allowing the kids to help me with menu planning makes them feel included, so they're happier to eat whatever I serve.

Have a set time range for evening meals

It's easy for my toddler and preschooler to be past their hungry time and not eat a proper meal because it's too late. Having an early time range (ours is from 5.00 pm to 5.30 pm) means the younger children will actually eat their dinner more often.

Eat at the table

I find it's much easier to get my children to focus on their meal if they're sitting up at a table. It's less tempting for small children to wander off and play with toys mid meal, and it also provides the best scenario for teaching children the social etiquette of eating a meal with others.

Get the children to help you

It's important for children to understand the work that goes into preparing the family meal. If they each have a small job to do, they become more involved and aware of the process.

Serve age-appropriate portions

About eleven years ago I went to a parenting seminar on eating and toilet training for toddlers, run by Tweddle Child and Family Health Services. They suggested when you serve up meals for a toddler, halve what you originally put on their plate and then halve it again. This is more likely to be an age-appropriate serve for a toddler. This was fantastic advice and has worked well for us. Toddlers who are hungry will ask for more, but

(continued)

Enjoying your mealtimes *(cont'd)*

they can be overwhelmed by large amounts of food on their plate. It also makes me feel better when I see an empty bowl.

Turn off distractions

I love having music on around the house, but even that must go off at mealtimes as it can easily distract the children. I also let any phonecalls go through to message bank so I'm not distracted by leaving the table. On occasion, when I'm tempted to answer a call, I always end up regretting it. The younger kids lose focus on the meal and it's impossible to get them to regain it.

Model appropriate behaviour

Children will follow the example set for them, so I always try to model the behaviour that I would like them to replicate. I'm not crazy about a number of vegetables, but setting the right example means eating those vegetables without complaint!

Encourage conversation

Mealtime is my greatest source of information about what's going on at school and kinder. The kids have had time to unwind and have relaxed a bit, so I find open-ended questions such as 'What did you play at lunchtime?', or 'Who did you play with at kinder?' encourage the kids to start telling me interesting stories about their day.

Remove the battlelines

Just as you can't make a baby sleep, I don't think you can make a child eat either. I've learned that getting kids to eat a meal can be a real battle. Spending time and money cooking a healthy meal only for it to be rejected and uneaten is incredibly frustrating. To make mealtimes enjoyable in our house, no-one is forced to eat their dinner; however, there's no substitute meal if they don't like what's been served: they'll have to wait until breakfast for something to eat.

Only focus on the big issues

To keep the tone of the evening meal light, I try not to comment on every single thing each child does that's not ideal. If I did, some nights that would be the only talking going on. I have core behaviours that I expect the children to meet and I monitor those, but if they accidentally slurp their spaghetti, or if the younger ones use their hands occasionally when trying to cut up their food, I let these go. Too much negativity can bring the mood down and close off conversation.

Try to teach table manners from an early age and introduce forks, spoons and knives (blunt butter knives are great) so that they are a normal part of eating.

Lou Woods, mum of four

Letting the family cook

In the monthly menu-planning template, one evening meal per week is set aside for my husband or the kids to cook. This wasn't always the case, so having a night off from cooking is a great break for me.

The change also didn't happen overnight. It evolved as my blogging workload increased and the children grew older. The benefits of giving the family a chance to do the cooking are not only mine either. My husband is now far more capable in the kitchen and has increased the selection of meals he can cook from five to about ten. My eldest son—who has begun cooking meals on his own—has more self-confidence and is building on his independence skills. To get your family involved in the kitchen with less of a fight, you should set expectations, familiarise your family with the kitchen and find child-friendly recipes.

Setting expectations

I first needed to work out what assistance I wanted with cooking the evening meals. How often did I want someone else to cook, and who did I think could do this? My husband and I discussed his involvement and we agreed on him being solely responsible for the meal on Saturdays and assisting on Sundays. Having clear expectations set up between us meant we each had our accountabilities. He was to cook the meal and I was to leave him in peace to do it, without constantly looking over his shoulder.

We then had a similar conversation with our eldest son. We had just begun teaching him to cook, so we then talked about how often he could cook a meal for the family on his own. We all agreed on once a month.

Introducing the family to the kitchen

Not everyone feels comfortable in the kitchen, but that doesn't have to be an excuse for keeping them out of it. I've witnessed how practice and familiarity can make a big difference in cooking a meal. To introduce my husband and my kids to the kitchen I've used a very similar process.

- *Health and safety lessons.* The kids are in the kitchen quite a bit with me, so it's valuable to remind them of kitchen safety and health basics such as:

  - washing hands

  - tying hair back

  - power-point and electricity safety

  - how to face pot handles

  - how to handle knives

  - cutting away from yourself.

- *Start small.* A gradual introduction is easier than jumping in the deep end. Starting the kids with small cooking projects such as scones, muffins and slices, and then progressing to light meals such as scrambled eggs, builds their confidence through success. They're then willing to try more complex recipes.

- *Watch and learn.* Just being in the kitchen and watching how things are done is really helpful. When learning how to prepare a meal, my husband prefers to watch me cook it in its entirety. He writes notes on a copy of the recipe while I'm cooking so he'll feel confident about cooking the meal by himself.

- *Doing it together.* The kids learn by watching me prepare a meal. The next time we prepare that dish the children cook it with me. This time they're in charge of the cooking and I supervise and answer any questions. This stage can take a while to perfect. For example, my eldest son only needs help once with some meals. However, for other, more complex recipes he may need me around a few times before he feels comfortable cooking it on his own.

- *Going solo.* Once they feel confident about cooking a meal, I let the kids be solely responsible for putting it together—from the first steps of finding the ingredients, to serving it and cleaning up. It can be tempting to step in and correct anything you see that might not be right. Sometimes I find it easier to walk away! I try not to intervene unless there's a safety issue involved. Kids tend to learn best from making mistakes and working things out by themselves.

Recipes for kids to cook

Table 2.3 shows some examples of recipes that my children and my 'non-cook' husband prepare for the family. All the recipes listed can be found on the blog at www.planningwithkids.com/family-friendly-recipes.

Family-friendly food

Not every meal I serve up for dinner is received joyfully by all my kids. Each child has their own distinct set of likes and dislikes. The kids have input to the menu plan, so their preferences are taken into account, but as the parent I also endeavour to expose them to new foods, textures and combinations. I've learned through many rejections and wasted meals that while trying to do this, I still need to keep an emphasis on making the food for our evening meals family-friendly.

Table 2.3: recipes for kids and partners to cook

Appropriate for	Recipes
3–5 year olds (with help)	■ Scones ■ Muffins ■ Chocolate balls ■ Vegemite scrolls ■ Traffic-light sandwiches
6–9 year olds (independently after practice)	■ Homemade pizza ■ Homemade chips (oven baked) ■ Scrambled eggs ■ Egg and bacon tarts ■ 100s of biscuits
10–12 year olds (independently after practice)	■ Tacos ■ Sausages and salad ■ Tuna rice ■ Spaghetti bolognaise ■ Banana cake
'Non-cook' partner	■ Beef stir-fry ■ Fried rice ■ Baked penne with bacon ■ Souvlaki ■ Chicken lasagne

Getting kids to eat

We've modified our approach to eating meals over the years. Originally, we used to offer the kids dessert after every meal and this often became a bargaining element. I remember saying things like, 'Eat three more bites, then you can have dessert', particularly if I was getting them to try something new. But as the children grew older, they'd ask, 'What's for dessert?' to find out whether it was worth eating those extra spoonfuls or not. Mealtime could become a battle over how much more was to be eaten.

To avoid this scenario, we agreed at a family meeting that we'd have dessert only twice a week, and the children would get to eat it regardless of whether they'd eaten their main meal or not. This was under the explicit understanding that once mealtime finishes there's no further option of eating food for the rest of the evening. If the children choose not to eat their meal, I don't discuss it with them other than to explain that it's their decision and that they'll have to wait until breakfast for something to eat.

There are nights when, after not eating their meal, one of the kids will say they're hungry. This comes mainly from the younger ones, as the older three don't bother telling me anymore. When I respond I aim to be empathetic and calm, and I explain they can have breakfast in the morning. This doesn't always end quietly or without tears; however, it happens infrequently as the kids have now grown used to the consequences of not eating their dinner.

Meals kids love

It's possible to serve up meals that are healthy *and* that kids will love. While the kids do have different preferences, self-serve meals tend to be winners. These are the types of meals where you set food out on the table and everyone selects what they want.

We have a number of different styles of self-serve meals like this, but the format is same: a serving of meat and a selection of pre-cut vegetables and salads to choose from. I find with these meals the kids eat more fresh vegetables. They're empowered by choice and they particularly love using little serving tongs to serve themselves.

Another bonus with these types of self-serve meals is that I generally have at least one child in the kitchen helping me prepare the food: slicing cheese, peeling carrots, tearing lettuce and cutting capsicum are all tasks that can easily be done by little hands.

Some self-serve meals that my kids love are:

- tacos
- chicken schnitzel and salad
- homemade hamburgers and salad
- pan-fried fish with salad
- salad rolls
- sausages and salad
- souvlaki
- baked potatoes
- chicken wings, corn and baked potatoes.

You can find these recipes on my blog at www. planningwithkids. com/family-friendly-recipes. We generally have one self-serve meal a week, which is always warmly received by the kids.

School lunches

One of the highlights of school holidays for me is not having to make school lunches. I find this task one of those repetitive and boring—although essential—ones of parenting: a perfect task for which to create a process!

Creating a school lunchbox process

School mornings can be stressful if there's too much to do and too much to think about. Our school lunchbox process streamlines the workload and takes the mental energy out of thinking about what to give the kids.

- *Establish how much food you need.* Through trial and error I've worked out how much food my children need to get them through the day. My seven-year-old daughter, for example, eats much less than her 12-year-old brother, so this is one thing I consider when packing the lunchboxes.

- *Create a school lunchbox guide.* Once I know how much food is enough for each child, I build a guide to refer to when making the school lunches. Having a guide also makes it easier to delegate this task to someone else—such as my husband—as the need arises. I find that five to six items (my daughter only needs five) from a good mix of food groups such as those listed here is enough for my children:

  - a core lunch item

  - a whole piece of fruit

  - veggie sticks

  - cut fruit

  - a home-baked treat

  - a selection of crackers or dried fruit.

- *Prepare as much as you can the night before.* Much of the preparation for school lunches can be completed the night before. Table 2.4 shows some examples.

Table 2.4: night-time lunchbox preparation

Item	Task
Fruit and vegetables	Cut up fruit and vegetables and store in fridge. I find that watermelon, rockmelon, strawberries and so on can be cut the night before and placed in airtight containers until morning.
Sandwiches	Cut up fresh ingredients for sandwiches if required. I like to make fresh sandwiches every day, purely as a personal preference. Some people are happy to make up large batches of sandwiches and freeze them in advance. I often grate carrot, shred lettuce, slice tomato and so on the night before so that I only have to make up the sandwich in the morning.

Item	Task
Dry snacks	Make up cracker and dried-fruit packs and place them in lunchbox.
Treats	Wrap up cake or muffins and place in lunchbox.

- *Have a regular baking day/s.* I've found that having a regular baking day helps ensure there's a home-cooked treat in the children's school lunches. Throughout most of the year I have one to two baking sessions per week: one on Sunday evening (which I do quickly by myself) and another on a week day, when I bake with our toddler and preschooler. I have a number of 'go to' recipes for making snacks for the kids' lunchboxes. These recipes are super easy to make and produce a generous amount so they last a few days. Some of my kids' favourites are:

  - banana cake

  - white chocolate-chip muffins

  - Anzac biscuits

  - 100s of biscuits.

You can find these on the blog at www.planningwithkids.com/family-friendly-recipes.

> Keep unbaked biscuit dough in the freezer—works a treat. I often prepare vast amounts at once and freeze the cookie dough in rolls. I can then just get it out, slice it, bake it and we have fresh biscuits.

Marita Beard, mum of two, www.leechbabe.com

Inspiring lunchbox ideas

With more than 200 school days in a year, it can be easy to run out of ideas for what to put into the kids' lunchboxes. So, as you can see in table 2.5 (overleaf), I created a 'cheat sheet' for two weeks' worth of ideas as a guide for inspiration.

Table 2.5: lunchbox inspiration cheat sheet

Item	Monday	Tuesday	Wednesday	Thursday	Friday
Week 1					
Core lunch item	Salad sandwich	Vegemite sandwich	Salad wrap	Ham sandwich	Vegemite sandwich
Whole fruit	Apple	Apple	Apple	Apple	Apple
Veggie sticks	Red capsicum	Cucumber	Red capsicum	Carrot	Celery
Fruit pieces	Watermelon	Grapes	Watermelon	Grapes	Strawberries
Crackers	Water crackers	Rice cakes	Cruskits	Vita-Weats	Rice cakes
Home-baked Treat	Banana cake	Banana cake	Banana cake	Chocolate balls	Chocolate balls
Week 2					
Core lunch item	Cold lamb sandwich	Cold lamb sandwich	Vegemite sandwich	Salad sandwich	Salad sandwich
Whole fruit	Pear	Apple	Pear	Apple	Pear
Veggie sticks	Snow peas	Green beans	Snow peas	Green beans	Carrot
Fruit pieces	Mandarin	Orange	Kiwi fruit	Mandarin	Orange
Crackers	Rice cakes	Cruskits	Rice cakes	Cruskits	Water crackers
Home-baked treat	Banana cake	Banana cake	Banana cake	Chocolate cake	Chocolate cake

Essential kitchen appliances

There are many small appliances and storage containers you can buy for the kitchen that are supposed to make life easier when it comes to preparing meals. You probably don't need half of them, and it can be difficult to find somewhere to store the bulky appliances. I now have a core that I use regularly and highly recommend to other families:

- *Slow cooker.* I was given one as a wedding present and didn't actually use it for six years. Now I use it almost weekly and love it. It helps you get evening meals ready in the morning with minimal fuss.

- *Large double steamer.* This is perfect for cooking large quantities of steamed vegetables and for making vegetable meals for babies when they start solids.

- *Rice cooker.* A rice cooker provides a very quick and easy way to cook large quantities of rice.

- *Large electric frypan.* I choose a non-stick frypan as I find with the heavy usage ours gets, the pan's lifetime is longer. We've found non-stick pans deteriorate quickly (especially if you put them in the dishwasher).

- *Large stockpot.* This is ideal for making large batches of soup or cooking up bulk amounts of pasta.

- *Fridge storage containers.* The secret to keeping fruit and vegetables fresh for the week is not using the crisper sections of the fridge. We keep all fruit and vegetables in specifically designed fridge containers that keep them fresher for much longer periods of time.

- *Pantry storage containers.* These are the most efficient and organised way to store baking goods such as flour, sugar, desiccated coconut and cocoa.

- *Electric mixer.* I'd love a flashy stand mixer, but it's not necessary for the type of cooking I do now. A hand-held electric mixer easily meets my needs.

- *Hand blender.* This is essential for making the kids' favourite soup (pumpkin) and handy for blending food when introducing solids to baby.

Taking action

- Start menu planning.

- Use the monthly menu plan template as a guide for helping build your menu plan.

- Add checklists to your pantry cupboards to keep track of items that need to be replaced.

- Create a shopping routine that allows you to purchase quality produce for the best price.

- Plan and prepare for mealtimes to make them a more enjoyable part of the day.

- Allocate cooking duties to your partner and kids to share the mealtime workload.

- Create a 'family favourites' list of meals that everyone loves as a handy menu-planning reference.

- Create a school lunchbox guide to make the daily task of preparing school lunches easier and more automated.

- Start lunchbox preparation the night before to take the pressure off busy school mornings.

- Allocate a regular time for baking. It makes filling lunchboxes with healthy food so much easier.

- Have the right equipment to make cooking healthy food for your family as easy as possible.

Chapter 3

Family finances

Every parent knows that as your family expands and as children grow, so do the family expenses. There are certain times during the year when I feel we're haemorrhaging cash. The beginning of school terms in particular can be difficult, with payments for after-school activities due, new clothes needed for the change of season and many utility bills also due around this time.

The family budget

Setting up a family budget was the best thing we did to stay on top of our finances. We've been running a family budget since we dropped to one income about eight years ago.

Budgeting is an ongoing activity for us that requires regular review to accommodate expansion and growth. It isn't a task we complete once and forget. As circumstances and requirements alter, the changes in income (hopefully up) and expenses (definitely up) need to be factored in so it truly reflects the household's finances.

Why family budgets work

I'm often asked if building and maintaining a family budget is worth the time it takes. Absolutely, it is! Budgets centralise the information needed to keep the finances under control and they work because they do the following:

- *Determine the cash available for spending.* Unless you sit down and calculate total expenses and incoming monies, you really are spending blindly.

- *Let you prioritise the family spending.* Rarely are there enough funds for all the purchases you would like to make. Assessing this up-front means you can choose what are the most important areas you need to allocate funds to.

- *Highlight where your money is being spent.* With cheques, credit cards, cash and regular direct debits, it can be difficult to get a feeling for where all your money is going, unless you track spending.

- *Help limit unnecessary expenses.* Budgeting and tracking where you spend your money is like having a second voice: Do I really need this? Is there room in the budget for this?

- *Create habits to enable savings.* Once you start budgeting, it quickly becomes evident how even small changes add up over time and can help to build up your savings. I find this really encourages me to keep going and meet a specific goal so we can have that family holiday or buy the new couch.

- *Provide an example to the kids of financial responsibility.* Children are heavily influenced by what they see. If all they see is spending, without the backdrop of a budget, they may get a distorted reality of how household finances work.

How to set a family budget

The easiest way to set a family budget is to break it down into a series of concrete steps (see figure 3.1).

1 Record all sources of income and expenses (fixed and variable) on the basis of frequency and amount.

2 Determine an annual savings goal (revisit step 1 if necessary).

3 Track daily spending.

4 Review progress of performance (revisit step 1 if necessary).

Figure 3.1: family budget flow chart

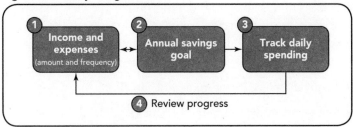

It helps to work on these steps one at a time so you don't feel overwhelmed by all the information to be collected. A simple spreadsheet is an effective tool for organising this information. Microsoft's Excel package is the most well-known brand of spreadsheet, but if you don't have access to it there's a range of free online versions available on the internet, such as Google Docs. Google Docs is a really effective tool for tracking spending across multiple locations (work and home) and across multiple people (both parents).

What helps us a lot is [that] my partner has another spreadsheet as well as the family budget. It tracks the progress on our mortgage (payments made, interest charged, and how far ahead we are of the bank's 'scheduled' total). The second motivates a keen adherence to the first, because money we preserve by keeping to our budget goes straight off the mortgage in almost all cases and we can SEE the benefit of that very clearly.

Kathryn Sinclair, mum of three, www.playeatlearnlive. blogspot.com

The basis of this approach to budgeting is to review the whole year, then break down the regular components on the basis of amount and frequency. This ensures you have enough cash to do the following:

- Enjoy the lifestyle you want and can afford.

- Put some away for a rainy day (for example, if the fridge has a heart attack or for an annual holiday) and to cover the 'lumpy' periods in the year.

You can find a template for a family budget spreadsheet at www. planningwithkids.com/resources. The template allows you to enter and record your income and expenses (step 1), target an annual savings goal (step 2) and track daily spending (step 3).

Step 1: estimate your income and expenses

Income: You need to estimate the total income for the year. This figure needs to include all sources of income, such as paid employment, government benefits, and returns on any

investments the family receives and their frequency, as shown in table 3.1.

Table 3.1: income (example figures)

	INPUT amount	INPUT frequency	Yearly total
Salary (or wage)	$2500	26	$65000
Family benefits (social security)	$100	12	$1200

If you have a regular salaried income, the process for entering the regular after-tax income multiplied by the period is very simple ($500 × 52 weeks, or $1000 × 26 weeks, or $2167 × 12 months). If your salary varies a lot from week to week, consider an average amount you believe to be realistic, or a minimum amount (if you want to be ultra conservative). If your income is seasonal, include the number of weeks you work multiplied by the amount ($700 × 12 weeks, for example).

Expenses (fixed): Recording your expenses takes more time than recording your income because we all have many expense transactions over the course of a week, month or year. While some expenses are fixed and some are variable, it will probably surprise you to see how many fit into the former category, and how large they are as well.

The first step is to detail all the fixed payments you have throughout the year. These costs define your financial life. If you purchase a $10 bunch of roses every week, this should be included in your budget. If purchasing a coffee every morning is a mandatory, not-negotiable, must-have event in your day, then include $3.50 every day for 365 days a year. (However, if you *occasionally* purchase a second coffee, this will need to be recorded as variable spending.)

With utility spending (such as gas, electricity and phone), many providers have offers for 'smoothing' seasonal bills. This makes the budgeting process and cash flow easier. However, if these bills can't be smoothed, have a look at your bills for the past 12 months. For example, if you spent $300 on gas bills last winter, then it's highly likely you'll spend a similar amount this winter. If the actual figure is 10 per cent more, that's when step 2 (determining an annual savings goal) is used to accommodate the uncertainties. If you don't have last year's records and you want to complete your budget now, you can either call your provider for this information or make an estimate and then update your budget as you receive the bills. Understanding the large items is important so you can manage the smaller, variable expenses with confidence.

Table 3.2 (see pp. 60–61) shows how your fixed expenses might look. Once you've calculated your yearly fixed expenses, you have a figure that will help determine what your maximum variable (discretionary) spending can be. The figure highlighted in bold in table 3.2 is then included in your net yearly savings calculations (see table 3.3 on p. 62) to determine what your maximum weekly variable spending amount must be if you want to achieve your yearly savings goal. If this figure is positive, hooray for you! If you stick to your budget you'll save money in that year. If it's negative and your expenses are higher than your income for the year, there are three options available to you:

- Dip into your savings.

- Pull back on some of your fixed or variable spending.

- Find some way of increasing your income.

Expenses (variable): Your variable expenses are all of the other things (apart from your fixed, regular expenses) you spend your money on. They include groceries, clothes, petrol, entertainment, children's activities, that second takeaway coffee and much more. It's difficult to categorise each of these expenses individually, so to keep it simple we use three core discretionary expenditure categories. It's important to keep this simple so that completing the third budgeting step — tracking daily spending — is a quick and easy task. We use these categories:

- *Groceries.* As well as food, this also includes nappies, toiletries and any additional items bought from the supermarket.

- *Miscellaneous expenses.* This is the catch-all category for those expenses that don't fit into the groceries or clothes categories. It includes things such as out-of-pocket medical expenses, babysitting, petrol, takeaway coffees, takeaway dinners and swimming lessons.

- *Clothes.* This is the category where you'll see the most variation because it's not a regular weekly expenditure. In our family we tend to buy clothes at the change of seasons and in bulk.

Table 3.2: fixed expenses (example figures)

	Total	Jul.	Aug.	Sep.	Oct.	Nov.	Dec.	Jan.	Feb.	Mar.	Apr.	May	Jun.
Utilities													
Water	$400			$100			$100			$100		$100	
Telephone	$1000			$250			$250			$250			$250
Gas and electricity	$1080	$90	$90	$90	$90	$90	$90	$90	$90	$90	$90	$90	$90
Internet	$420	$35	$35	$35	$35	$35	$35	$35	$35	$35	$35	$35	$35
Financial													
Mortgage (or rent)	$12 000	$1000	$1000	$1000	$1000	$1000	$1000	$1000	$1000	$1000	$1000	$1000	$1000
Accountant fees	$250								$250				
Bank fees	$300						$300						
Pocket money	$480	$40	$40	$40	$40	$40	$40	$40	$40	$40	$40	$40	$40
Education													
School fees	$800	$200			$200				$200			$200	
Kinder fees	$1440		$360			$360			$360			$360	
Insurance													
Car	$600							$600					
House	$300		$300										
Contents	$550		$550										
Health	$2400	$200	$200	$200	$200	$200	$200	$200	$200	$200	$200	$200	$200

	Total	Jul.	Aug.	Sep.	Oct.	Nov.	Dec.	Jan.	Feb.	Mar.	Apr.	May	Jun.
Travel													
Car registration	$500							$500					
Car maintenance	$400			$400									
Auto club	$75	$75											
Public transport	$1200	$100	$100	$100	$100	$100	$100	$100	$100	$100	$100	$100	$100
Miscellaneous													
Newspaper	$240	$20	$20	$20	$20	$20	$20	$20	$20	$20	$20	$20	$20
Milk delivery	$480	$40	$40	$40	$40	$40	$40	$40	$40	$40	$40	$40	$40
Dog fees	$40									$40			
Rates	$800		$200			$200			$200			$200	
Gym membership	$720	$60	$60	$60	$60	$60	$60	$60	$60	$60	$60	$60	$60
Presents — general	$636	$53	$53	$53	$53	$53	$53	$53	$53	$53	$53	$53	$53
Presents — Christmas	$1000						$1000						

$28 105 ← This figure links into the 'Net yearly savings' worksheet (see table 3.3 on p. 62).

It can appear incorrect to define groceries as a variable expense because we all have to eat. When shopping for groceries, however, there is considerable choice as to what we buy, how much we buy and where we buy from. Therefore, we use our discretion to make the purchases that are right for our family. For example, the chocolates that make their way regularly onto my shopping list are completely discretionary. I could definitely live without them! I don't want to though, so I buy them and they form part of my grocery spending.

The most effective way to determine the budget for variable expenses is to note all your discretionary expenditure over a few weeks. Write down everything, come up with a 'best guess' of what you will spend, and then multiply this by a frequency of 52 weeks for the year.

Table 3.3: net yearly savings (example figures)

	INPUT amount	INPUT frequency	Yearly total
Income			
Salary (or wage)	$2500	26	$65000
Family benefits (social security)	$100	12	$1200
Investments	$500	12	$6000
			$72200
Expenses			
Regular payments (i.e. bills, train fares, insurances)	$28105	1	$28105
Groceries	$275	52	$14300
Miscellaneous expenses	$275	52	$14300
Clothes	$100	52	$5200
			$61905
Net yearly savings (or deficit)			**$10295**

Step 2: determine your yearly savings goal

In the first step we determined our income and our fixed and variable expenses. The next step is to plan for future expenditure. Once all of these items have been entered, the spreadsheet calculates the net yearly savings (or deficit). In table 3.3, the result is $10 295 in savings. This is generally not the case the first time you put together a budget.

When we did our first budget, we estimated a significant deficit. This really scared me. It became very clear I was on a spending path that was going to get us into financial trouble. It was the small things that added up: morning tea with friends, magazines, buying 'on-sale' clothing. Setting a budget didn't mean I couldn't spend money on these things, but it did teach me that I needed to make more considered decisions.

To reduce the estimated deficit, we looked at all of our expenses and worked out where we could make cuts. We had to make changes to our lifestyle to do this. For the first couple of years our goal was simply to break even.

Knowing your forecast financial situation is incredibly useful. If you wanted to save for a home deposit or a new car, you may need a $10 000 surplus to achieve your goal. Through the budget-setting process you can determine the areas of spending you need to reduce or eliminate. You're then aware of any lifestyle changes you need to make, which ultimately makes achieving your financial goals much more likely. The hardest part of the budget process is setting it up the first time. Adjusting the budget for the changes in your life is much simpler from then on.

Step 3: track your daily spending

For budgeting to be effective, you need to now match your well-researched and considered set of numbers with the discipline to track your spending and review your performance. Without this, a budget is just a meaningless set of numbers on a page.

My husband and I both access a computer most days so entering every transaction into the tracking worksheet is convenient for us. This is where Google Docs is incredibly flexible. We uploaded our spreadsheet to Google Docs and we can access it on any computer with internet access. However, you don't have to use a computer to track expenditure. For the first year or two of tracking our expenses, we handwrote all expenses on a printed pro-forma spreadsheet and then added up the totals weekly.

A template for tracking daily expenditure is shown in table 3.4 (see pp. 66–67) and in the family budget spreadsheet found at www.planningwithkids.com/resources. There you'll also find a link to a Google Docs spreadsheet template.

In table 3.4 you can see just how quick and easy it is to start running a deficit. This is especially the case when you first begin the tracking process. We do our grocery shopping monthly, but the budget is based on weekly expenditure. This means our weekly spending varies quite significantly on paper for expenses such as groceries and clothes. It's much better to look at the overall trend of the budget. If we're simply adding to the deficit every week, then something is wrong and needs to be addressed.

Personally, the greatest benefit of regularly tracking our expenses is that it makes me think twice about spending our money. For example, the first week in table 3.4 shows a deficit of $425. This information allows me to make a considered decision. I wouldn't choose that weekend to take the kids to the movies. Instead, we might have a movie night at home: watch a DVD with popcorn and rearrange the lounge room to make it more special.

It's also important not to run a zero balance each week. For example, the allocation for clothing in the table is $100 a week, but, in reality, this is not how expenditure on clothes works. A new suit for my husband or replenishing the school uniforms at the start of the year costs significantly more than the weekly allocation. In the weeks leading up to purchasing these items, we need to start building a surplus to keep the budget on track.

Step 4: review your progress

By entering your daily spending, you can instantly view the health of your budget. In addition, it's important to review your overall budget regularly to make sure it remains relevant and realistic, and that it addresses any areas of overspending. When we first started budgeting, we would review our budget each quarter. Some of our initial estimates on spending in areas such as groceries weren't reflecting reality. We were spending at least $50 a week more than we thought we had been. We allocated more money to the budget for groceries, but as the budget was only just balanced, we had to find somewhere to take the money from. It came from miscellaneous expenditure. This then meant a further tightening up on things such as those extra coffees here and there, beginning to handmake gifts for people, and changing our newspaper delivery to weekends only.

Now we review the budget during the year on an as-needs basis. Over the years we've been able to accurately estimate our spending on groceries and clothes. The 'miscellaneous' category continues to be the trickiest one to balance as it covers expenditure on unpredictable costs. By having a budget, and tracking and reviewing our progress, it's been possible for us to reduce our debt to only having a mortgage while still buying the essential, additional big items (such as a fridge) when we need them and taking the occasional family holiday!

Table 3.4: tracking daily spending (example figures)

| 2011 | Input daily spend here ($) | | | Variance to budget ($) | | | | |
	Misc.	Groceries	Clothes	275 Misc.	275 Groceries	100 Clothes	Total	
Mon, 2 May	10	400						
Tue, 3 May	107	6						
Wed, 4 May		12	50					
Thu, 5 May	10							
Fri, 6 May	300			527	498	50	1075	Week total
Sat, 7 May	80	60		-252	-223	50	-425	Variance to budget
Sun, 8 May	20	20		-252	-223	50	-425	Total position (... this is the most important number)
Mon, 9 May	13	22						
Tue, 10 May	80							
Wed, 11 May	12							
Thu, 12 May		6						
Fri, 13 May	40			145	88	0	233	Week total
Sat, 14 May		60		130	187	100	417	Variance to budget
Sun, 15 May				-122	-36	150	-8	Total position (... this is the most important number)

2011	Input daily spend here ($)			Variance to budget ($)			
	Misc.	Groceries	Clothes	275 Misc.	275 Groceries	100 Clothes	Total
Mon, 16 May		430					
Tue, 17 May	22	15					
Wed, 18 May		7					
Thu, 19 May	50						
Fri, 20 May				72	512	200	784	Week total
Sat, 21 May		60	200	203	−237	−100	−134	Variance to budget
Sun, 22 May				81	−273	50	−142	Total position (... this is the most important number)
Mon, 23 May		32					
Tue, 24 May	90						
Wed, 25 May	80	6					
Thu, 26 May	30						
Fri, 27 May		6		225	104	0	329	Week total
Sat, 28 May	25	60		50	171	100	321	Variance to budget
Sun, 29 May				131	−102	150	179	Total position (... this is the most important number)

Managing pocket money

You might have noticed in table 3.2 (see pp. 60–61) that one of the fixed expenses we budget for is pocket money for the kids. This is not a necessity, but we made a decision that we would give pocket money to our kids to teach them practical finance lessons such as:

- *the value of money:* for example, understanding the cost of items and toys

- *decision making:* how best to use their limited funds

- *saving:* setting themselves goals—both short- and long-term—for how they'll spend their money

- *not being influenced by advertising:* when they see something in a catalogue or on TV and they say they want to spend their pocket money on it, this is the perfect opportunity to explain the purpose of advertising, and how to question what they're hearing and reading

- *social etiquette:* learning to be discreet about their earnings and being grateful for what they receive.

Pocket-money guidelines

When we decided we'd give our children pocket money, I did quite a bit of research. I wanted to understand the different models used and to find one that would fit in with our parenting style.

As with most parenting information, I found many pocket-money models, so our model is a hybrid of what I liked best about the various models I read about. In short, this is what my husband and I came up with.

- We would hand out pocket money fortnightly.

- It would be given out at the end of family meetings. If we missed a family meeting for some reason, the kids would receive the owed money at the next meeting.

- The amount would differ according to the children's ages.

- Once they reached school age, each child would get an increase. The additional amount was to be deposited into their school bank account.

- The children may not spend their money until they've saved $20.

- The children may choose how to spend their money.

- Pocket money is not related to their allocated jobs around the house.

When to start giving pocket money

We chose to start giving our eldest son pocket money when he started school at age five. Before that we didn't feel he needed his own supply of cash! However, we started giving our second son a very small amount of pocket money after he turned three so he wouldn't feel left out. This decision made shopping trips designed for spending pocket money much easier!

How much pocket money?

I don't think there is any 'right' amount to give kids in terms of pocket money. It's a relative issue determined by your family's income. I understand that for some families giving pocket money isn't even an option as there's simply no room for it in the budget. My biggest tip for handing out pocket money is to start small and make sure your family budget can cope with this regular payment.

I have a seven, nine and 11 year old. They [each] get $1 a week. Kids today get way too much—they buy, buy, buy. It's important for children to learn to save and consider their purchases, just like we have to.

Georgina Rechner, mum of three

It's also important to be clear on what we, as parents, don't expect the kids to have to spend their pocket money on. We give only a small amount of pocket money, but we pay for things such as the kids' trips out with friends and the occasional treat from the school canteen. Other families choose to give a much larger amount, but expect their kids to manage their money and pay for extra items as well.

Our eldest son started secondary school recently, and he takes public transport to school. We're going to trial the second method mentioned above as we think it's more appropriate for his circumstances and age. Parenting kids is a dynamic task requiring constant adaptation, modification and reality checks!

Spending pocket money
We'd agreed that the kids needed to save at least $20 before they could spend any money to ensure they didn't get caught up in constant consumerism and instant gratification. It also

meant they could buy one bigger item as opposed to a few smaller items. Stuff already accumulates so quickly in our house that we didn't want to exacerbate this even further.

We'd also agreed that the kids could choose what they spent their money on, but I admit to initially trying to influence their purchases. If they were looking at a commercialised toy that made noises and needed batteries, I would—not so innocently—try to distract their attention to an educational game! I didn't get away with this for very long as my eldest son, who was seven at the time, soon worked out what I was doing. He made it clear that it was 'my money and I get to decide'. He was right: if I was going to encourage responsible spending, I had to allow them to make their own choices.

The first year our kids were given pocket money, they bought a lot of plastic, junky toys. This was most likely a direct result of my not having ever bought these types of toys for them, and for a while it seemed it was all they were interested in.

However, I only had to put up with these toys for a relatively short time because allowing the kids to buy them actually resulted in a positive longer term outcome. As the kids grew older and become more experienced at spending their money, they worked out for themselves that these cheap, plastic toys weren't that great after all: they broke easily and many small parts were difficult to keep track of.

Once they learned this, the older kids started putting more thought into their purchases. They started setting savings goals of more than $20 because they had particular items in mind. The items they spend their pocket money on now are rarely toys. Books, cricket gear, a hammock and an umbrella are among the purchases they have planned and made.

Taking action

- Create a family budget.

- Use the budget template to help you determine your expenses and the level of savings you want to aim for.

- Begin tracking your daily expenditure, using either the template spreadsheet or a notebook.

- If you already have a budget in place, take the time to regularly review and modify it so it can help you meet your family's financial goals.

- Decide whether to give your kids pocket money.

- If you're going to give pocket money, spend time defining why you want to and create a process for doing so.

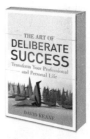